Published by Stratford Living Publishing.

ISBN Print: 978-1-990332-62-3

Dedicated to TJ

We're at the Amusement Park today!

We can't wait to have fun and play!

Amazing rides, food and plenty to do...

But I never thought I'd see an AARDVARK too!

It all happened when I lost my family...

And they weren't where they were supposed to be...

WAIT
HERE IF
YOU'RE LOST

So, I tried to be brave and look around...

That's when an AARDVARK in the Amusement Park is what I found!

He was a cheeky little mammal with a long, long nose...

He was kind of cute, I suppose.

But he was wearing sunglasses to block out the light...

That's because
aardvarks
are noctural - they
<u>usually</u> only
come out at night.

I followed him to the Ferris Wheel...

It wasn't my first ride, but if it was his - I wondered how he'd feel...

Aardvarks squeal - who knew????

Then it was time to...

JUMP JUMP JUMP...

BECAUSE THERE WAS
AN AARDVARK...

IN THE AMUSEMENT PARK!

He scampered away and I kept on his trail...

He sniffed the air -I knew he was on the candy floss trail!

I thought aardvarks only ate termites!

When he finished he ran toward the lights!

He jumped the line and went onto the roller coaster...

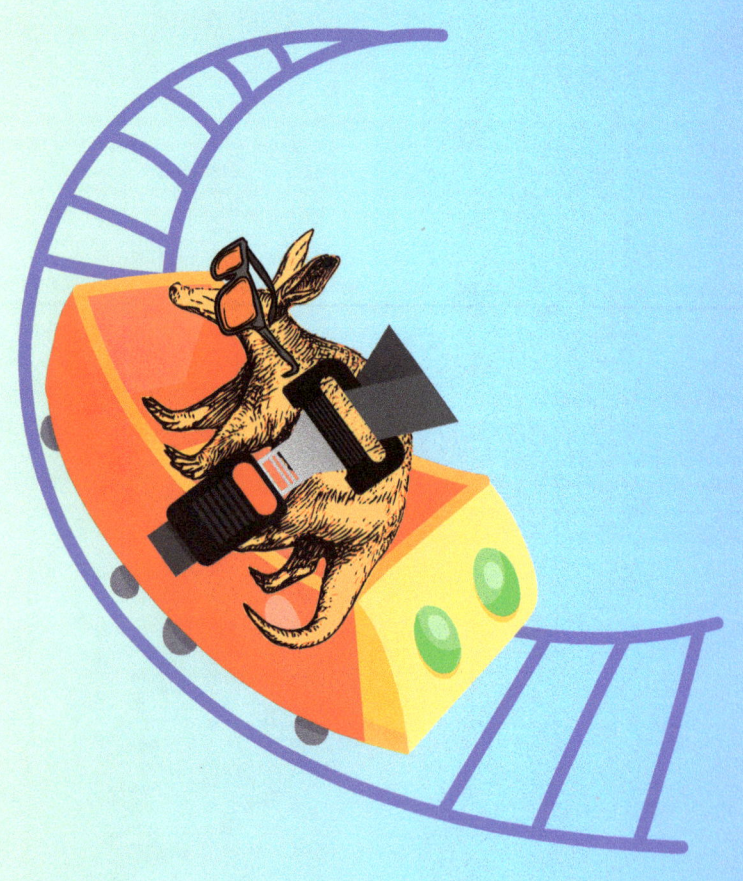

It was climbing higher and higher into the blue...

He turned with a grin as the cart dropped down...

Again it was time for me to...

JUMP JUMP JUMP...

BECAUSE THERE WAS AN AARDVARK

IN THE AMUSEMENT PARK!

Mommy, Daddy and my sister found me!

"Why weren't you at the meeting place?" asked Daddy.

I tried to explain..but the aardvark was gone...

SO, I JUMP JUMP JUMPED BECAUSE THERE WAS AN AARDVARK IN THE AMUSEMENT PARK.

As we walked on, I saw him going into the scary house!

"Let's go," my sister said. But I wasn't going in. I was too scared.

There was a scream, as
the aardvark ran out.

WE JUMP JUMP JUMPED BECAUSE THERE WAS AN AARDVARK IN THE AMUSEMENT PARK!

As he ran through the crowd...

Someone yelled, "HEY! No aardvarks allowed!"

Suddenly it felt like my head was in a cloud!

Then the aardvark left the Amusement Park..

amusement park

Without even saying goodbye!

And suddenly my tummy felt very weird!

Like I was going to cry!

A crowd gathered around...

But the aardvark could no longer be found!

WE JUMP JUMP JUMPED LIKE WE'VE NEVER JUMPED BEFORE...

BECAUSE THERE WASN'T AN AARDVARK

IN THE AMUSEMENT PARK ANYMORE!

WHO KNOWS WHAT FUN HE WAS HAVING NOW?

We

meeting an aardvark in the Amusement Park!

Other books in the
Jump Series:
Jump Like a Caribou!
Jump Like a Kangaroo!
Jump at the Zoo!
Jump and Say P.U.!
Jump and Say Boo!
Jump and Say Valentine's Day Is
For Kids Too!
Jump and Look For a Clue
Jump and Say Happy Birthday to
You!
Jump For Everything Blue!
Jump and Say Cock-A-Doodle-
Do!
Jump and Squawk Like A
Cockatoo!
Jump and Ask Is It You or Ewe?

Jump and Ask Is It You or Ewe?
Jump and Say There's an Ewww in My Stew!
Jump and Cheer Happy New Year!
Jump, Hop and Say Happy Easter To You!
Jump and Say There's A Moo-Moo In My Tutu!
Jump and Say There's a Hare in My Hair!

The Cat Who Said Hello
The Three Boulders
Billy Shakespeare
Billie Shakespeare

NON-FICTION
103 Fundraising Ideas For Parent Volunteers With Schools and Teams

www.ingramcontent.com/pod-product-compliance
Lightning Source LLC
Chambersburg PA
CBHW051556120626

46551CB00013B/1550